SECRET FORMULAS & TECHNIQUES OF THE MASTERS

SECRET FORMULAS & TECHNIQUES OF THE MASTERS

Jackie Craven

Brick Road Poetry Press
www.brickroadpoetrypress.com

Cover: Detail from *Lobster for Lunch* © Louise Craven Hourrigan

Author photo: © Adrianne Mathiowetz

Library of Congress Control Number: 2018959342
ISBN: 978-0-9979559-5-8

Published by Brick Road Poetry Press
513 Broadway
Columbus, GA 31902-0751
www.brickroadpoetrypress.com

Brick Road logo by Dwight New

Table of Contents

When the Last of Them Died

Maroger's Magic

The night before he left for the nursing home,
my stepfather called to tell me about the burglars
who slipped through his skylight, whisked away
the Portmeirion china, the vacuum cleaner,
and the four-poster bed—removed everything
without disturbing his blankets or his sleep.
Even your mother's paintings, he said, the one
with the goose, and that Mexican scene, and the still life
with the pomegranate spilling seeds so red
they'd make your tongue curl. He breathed softly
into the phone. Gone, just gone. Then: Well, not gone
completely. My stepfather believed that for every
item taken, the thieves left a replica. The smallest details,
down to the dent on the refrigerator door, had been
reproduced. But don't tell your sister, he whispered:
She's a duplicate, too. He would not be convinced
otherwise. And me? I still believed in the magic
potion my mother mixed with paint to give fruit
a lifelike luster, an amber jelly brewed
according to instructions from an out-of-print book
my sister and I rediscovered when we went to empty
our parents' house. Look, she said, cracking open the spine,
the recipe calls for mastic tears dissolved in turpentine
and simmered with smoked oil and white lead—
so expensive and toxic, and the temperature must be exact.
Who could possibly get it right? I swayed, dizzy
from the memory of steam billowing from an enamel pot,
a stench of burning walnuts, and then, jars crashing
into the garbage bin—the solvent spoiled. We sat
cross-legged beside the packing crates, children again,

as my sister read to me from *The Secret Formulas*
and Techniques of the Masters, written during World War II
by Jacques Maroger, a reactionary who, she gently explained,
must've been insane.

Without the Lights and Shadows

Without the lights and shadows
an object would make no
appearance to the eye.
                    —Jacques Maroger

Old Woman with Goose (30 x 24, Oil)

When I was a swirling minnow
my mother filled this canvas
with loam and olives—layer

after layer of brown aromas—
She must've felt queasy
perched on her artist stool,

swooping her palette knife
side to side while I swam
inside her. I learned

to walk on land and saw
how she glazed buff over
blue, dusk over amber—

colors stroked on, scraped away—
She couldn't make paint behave.
She wanted a Rubens scene

like the one that inspired Yeats—
wings, thighs, a shudder
in the loins. But the tossing

truth of me—moving, growing—
seasickness and a smell
of pee and turpentine,

and the strange heart
beating beneath her ribs.
Instead of Leda, she painted

an angry crone—knurled fingers
grasping a blur of white
feathers. I believe she'd like

to wring the bird's neck.
Those fierce eyes follow me
across the room.

House Beautiful Designer Room #132

You wonder who will fill the Barcelona chairs,
drink from tulip glasses, eat the peaches
in the starburst bowl. A Calder mobile turns,

casting slow shadows on parquet floors.
Tufted cushions hold their breath.
You press a damp finger to the photograph.

Beyond sliding doors, only daffodils,
an improbable sky, a smudge
from your inky hand.

1962, Polaroid

When Kennedy told us what the Russians planned
my mother said we were fortunate
to have a basement, although
she wasn't sure she could live underground
with my father. Where would he sleep?
The television played old news reels of Hiroshima
and a murder mystery by Alfred Hitchcock,
who was wide and bald like Khrushchev, but
did not threaten to incinerate the planet,
and who spoke with such a soothing British accent.
I drifted into dreams of butterbats,
which were nocturnal butterflies
with radioactive fur.

The sun rose. My mother poured orange juice
to help me grow. Her art students arrived
and propped their easels like teepees
on the patio. She set out cocktail tables
for their paints and brushes. We did not
eat our neighbor's dog. The sky turned
pale as ash, but hot, and the students perspired
inside their smocks. I carried jugs of water
to the basement. On a cot beneath a cloud
of cigarette smoke, my father snored
as though the world might never end.
From the garden, a student asked,
"How do you make wings?"

Glass, Iron, Feathers

Because my father would not allow a dog
my mother bought a parakeet
we called Firebird after the Stra-
vinsky ballet—griffin claws
backward knees butter-colored
zebra wings like a costume by
Marc Chagall—any moment
Firebird might shape-shift into
a sorceress and cast a spell—
Exorcizamus omnis immundus spiritus—
real birds aren't usually this articu-
late but some nights I could hear
wild ones shriek—rusty hinges—
shattered glass—mocking
birds mocking the whip-poor-
wills who called to the loons who
answered the hawks—
HeeEEEKYeeeAAAYAH—
and then the moonlight
and the scent of honeysuckle
and whiskey and dangerous dreams
floating on one long *eeee-oooow*—
smarter than any dog my mother said
and used her grocery money to buy
a parakeet training record—*Hel-lo-bay-bee*—
Firebird fluffed to twice her size and the record
went on and on—*Hel-looo-bay-beeeeeee*—her beak—
old-man toenail—opened wide enough to say *AKKK*
and my father said *What do you expect from a feather-brain?*—
a translucent eyelid slid sideways shutting like a shower door

and my mother opened the wire cage—*eeee-EEEEEEEEEE*—
a smudge of mustard on the air—the record turning—
Firebird turning and turning—window top to wing chair—
droppings like tear crusts on the walls—an origami bird
in a furious wind—my mother saying *baby-baby*—my father—
crazy-crazy—the record—*bay-beeeee*—and the parakeet swirling
yellow circles—Stravinsky voice trying to say *beeeeeeee*—

The Psychic Says

In your 394th life, you were a pond. You wanted to be a lake
and cried yourself to the brim, but the sun—

You came back an estuary. Not fresh, not salt.
Not land, not sea. Crabs tunneled through the mushy parts

of you. Always the threat of evaporation.
You dabbled in many incarnations—

Life 1,052, a fall (always falling). Life 6,893, a canal
(it was those locks that did you in).

In life 14,659 you managed to become an ocean.

You curled your lips at the sun and swallowed
Atlantis whole. No one guessed

how you dogged the moon or how you suffered
the sickening swirl of your perpetual motion. Now

you throw yourself up at my shore, thirsty
for answers. Seriously? I think you already know

why you weep, why you bleed, and why, as you drift
to sleep, you hear a steady hiss of steam.

I Heard a River Downstairs

Half-formed words hissed to the surface
and tried to walk on land. Silver-scaled whispers
swished from the kitchen, fizzled

down the hall, and swelled
in my parents' room. For a sleepy moment
I wondered whether my teacher, Miss Simmons,

had slipped into our home—a mission
to correct my lisp. *Repeat after me:*
Sun. Sky. Sorrow. But this was summer—

No lessons, no drills, only the hush
of grownups deep in mysterious discussion.
I stretched my ears into points, strained

to hear voices that slithered and hid behind
the summer noises—crickets rubbing thighs,
bullfrogs burping in the grass, cries so shrill

fireflies throbbed. A few stray Ss, snatches
of my name, swirled like candy wrappers
in the current. Miss Simmons always said

I tried too hard. She claimed I had sibilance
already inside me, waiting. *Clench your teeth*
and blow, she instructed. But as secrets

splashed against my window and seeped
beneath my door, my head felt heavy
and I forgot where to put my tongue.

To My Tongue

Flabby-bottomed bottom feeder,
blind slug, taster and teller of lies,
what am I to do with you?

There you loll, pimpled with pleasure,
dreaming of steamy croissants
and buttered kisses, leaving me

to wash the dishes. I feel you curl
in my cheek and lap at my teeth
and I'm reminded of the hermaphroditic

gastropods who slid into
my mother's garden, shape-shifted
their sexes and ate her hostas.

Meanwhile in the gazebo—
piña coladas and tiramisu,
voices rimmed with lipstick,

obstreperous casseroles.
Must you slobber on everything?
I've been thinking it might be time

for us to go our separate ways,
for you to grow gargoyle wings
and fly off to Taco Bell,

wafting halitosis, trailing crumbs.
But then—what of me? No words,
no wants? A castrato who cannot sing?

Cocktails on the Patio, 1964

Confetti people in Hawaiian prints drifted from the house
to find the roses overcome, swaying beneath the weight
of Japanese beetles. Copper wings, armor shells,

rainbow flecks. Wobbling on silver heels, my mother pushed
through thorns while liquid voices called—*Come!* Ice pinged
in glasses round as crystal balls. *Happy Hour!* Cicadas shrieked

from treetops. *Happy Hour!* Mother plucked the beetles
one by one. She tried not to tear roseflesh, but the barbed feet
held on. Her friends chittered, crickets in the grass. *Come join us!*

She scooped beetles by the handful—teeming clumps,
animated apricots—and put them in a jar of turpentine,
which should have killed them. Sunset shrilled with frog song,

ice crackled in aluminum trays, gypsy earrings glittered beneath
tiki torches. My mother's glass brimmed amber as she watched
beetles churn inside their jar. Laughter swelled, wild

and delirious. The cocktails, the ruined roses—a swirl
of fermentation, potent and irresistible.

Tempest in a Paintbox

All those little compartments, each one
containing a ghost—Van Gogh in his cell,
manic flowers, olive trees gone wild—
while Seurat tiptoes room to room, whispering

anxious pixels. To survive, they consume
rivers of absinthe—difficult for Chagall,
whose dreams are pure as a drowsy bride,
impossible for Pollock, who has already swallowed

too much blue. The noise. The smell.
Mondrian will surely go insane. Pacing
his cubicle, he measures heaven
(height—length—depth) and never considers

the plight of those who live below. Poor old
Dutch masters, reeking sepia and beer,
pondering where in their damp quarters
to hang the shadows.

Growing Faster Than Swamp Bamboo, My Mother Liked to Say

August turned our lake into a gloomy puddle
where minnows sank from the weight
of their own bodies and grownup voices
drifted on smoke from sad little charcoal fires
which made me wish for a cigarette—
a cloud of sin I could hold in my lungs
and no one would guess the darkness
inside me—or a secret tattoo
like a dragonfly or a message written in code—
impossible to decipher as I waded into the deepest
green. The water used to reach my chin but now
my legs were so much longer—
Even out by the rusty buoy
my feet touched bottom and mud pushed
between my toes. Above the din of lovelorn frogs
I heard her call and call.

The Strength of the Jelly

The strength of the jelly
is in direct proportion
to the amount of lead . . .
                    —Jacques Maroger

Carnival (Tempera on Cardboard)

A lopsided Ferris wheel pretends to turn
in this painting from sixty years ago. Carousel ponies
pause mid-gallop, banners stiffly wave,
and a marmalade sun shines a light that's not quite real
but brighter—darkly bright like patent leather,
a tune played by a mechanical monkey or an electric
glow from an adjoining room. A lamp turned on
when I cried for my mother, who painted this illusion
and who came trailing the scent of enchantment,
her spoon pinging as she stirred a magic potion
brewed especially for me—Rum laced with honey,
cinnamon, and fire.

The Absinthe Drinker (Egg Tempera & Oil)

The first sip flamed into another sip like a sun storm—
like an Olympic medal—like Pompeii—
like Pompeii before lava made love groan
beneath the weight of heat—Sweet Jesus! That sip
turned the scent of gasoline into the sound of tambourines—
My lips had been an iron gate—a Syrian desert
shriveled into a frown—My tongue a slug
curled in the hollow of my cheek—Hell
I was nothing but a hotel sign flapping on a rusty chain—
a fleabag room—curtains pursed—but that wet light flashed
like resurrection hollering hallelujahs—hit high notes
from the very first sip—shrill and trembling—
singing goddamn *Götterdämmerung*—
squeezing music out my pores till my skin
stretched to cellophane—That tight! That transparent!
Vesuvius spitting jalapeño breath—hot and bright
and dark too—dark on top—flames stoking underneath—
swirling me through a wormhole—time
swallowing its tail—blindness turned inside out—that sip—
If some Higher Power cracked the world open like an egg
and you felt your soul swim up from your ribs—
felt your soul rear on hind legs—a clash of crystal horses
rearing and charging and taking off on fourteen-foot wings—
Teratornis wings—God help me! One sip and I was melting
mountains into cream—Oh yeah! I lit the sky like a meteoroid—
an asteroid—a flaming Jabberwock! No bones. No skull.
Only eyes—nothing but eyes and a wide wet smile—

Beware the Pearly Gates

Pastors dangle heaven like a pilgrim's promise
to a trusting tribe. But, imagine the horror
of two dozen exes unfurling reproaches,

disappointed parents shaking bobbleheads,
angel ancestors tsking over silver harps.
How can there be bliss with so many people from our past

gathered like drunken relatives at Thanksgiving,
platters heaped with recriminations,
jellied secrets in fancy molds?

Forget the sermons. When Sunday comes,
let's linger between sweat-glistened sheets—
you, me, our delirious savage heat.

My Grandmother Won't Say Why She Jumped Off the Pier

in her party clothes
that moonlit December evening
my grandfather proposed.
For sixty years her secrets
floated out to sea.
When I beg for answers
she speaks only of salt and ice,
a swish of emerald water,
and the glint of ships
she could not reach
because my grandfather
seized her sash
and pulled her ashore.
Now that arthritis
has turned her hands to fists,
he pours her juice
and holds her straw.
As she drifts to sleep
he turns to me
and whispers: *Silly girl.*
Forgot she couldn't swim.

Still Life with Stuffed Olive

Silly Cyclops, amphibious friend, I'm on to you,
bebopping in your tight green skin,
ogling the cocktail onions. Oh yeah, my tongue
knows your nippled form, the circulean way
you tumble about, wafting the scent of coriander,
vermouth, and brine. *Swim!* you say,
your karaoke voice sloshing against the rim,
and indeed I would—swim all the way
to Athens or the Galapagos, splash
in the Angostura bitters, explore your tunnel
of deep forgetting. But, my naughty tadpole,
I've seen your salty somersaults,
watched the flicker of your pimento tail
become your clitoris, become your belly button,
become your mouth, become your eye,
become—What then? Night after night
you flit past my lips, singing *Fly Me
to the Moon*, only to dive for the crotch
of my nearly-empty glass, where—*every time!*—
you drink the last drop. The best drop—

Waiting for 5:00 at Bailey's Pub (Ink & Charcoal)

Happy Hour, my happiest Hour,
where are you now? Dancing naked

in Brazil, I suppose, or detained
in Colombia, setting licorice on fire.

Alone in the corner booth, I turn the pages
of my cocktail napkin. I see you glisten

in my coffee and think of you
in some other zone, time tossed with bitters

and a twist of lime. Do you remember
how we used to lick salt from the rim

of the equator? What did we care
about gestures of the sun?

My hands fold around the ghost
of your frosted glass.

Thirst

I promise him everything—rivers, falls,
Lake Saguaro—but he sniffs and turns away.

Weeping and pleading, I follow him
across the mesa. I fling my arms
around his hollow neck and he becomes a snarl
of tumbleweed.

His teeth are salt and heat has shrunk his eyes.
All he needs, I can give, and still
he hurtles into the yellow wind.

Flight (30 x 25, Oil on Canvas)

Printed on the back of the frame:
LAHEY A.M.

Perhaps Lahey is the room
where my mother took an early class

in abstraction, or a teacher who
introduced vermilion

and said *Let go*. How to decipher
the Fauvist strokes of a savage

palette knife? A James Lahey tweets,
I am Alcohol in the Flesh.

Another Lahey *turned to art*
late in life. Or did the obituary say

that in a wild departure from form,
the painter turned life late into art?

Blackbirds burst through flaming trees.

The Temperature Reaches 102

The North Pole is melting,
and Antarctica, and in Greenland
glaciers break away—
my own small garden fills
with black rain and the scent of mud
and fermentation, heavy aromas
from long ago: I'm a feverish child
at the top of the stairs, dreaming
my mother in the room below,
hearing the shush of her slippers
and a metallic ping—ice
in her glass or the clasp to the door
she opens wide enough to let the night
whoosh in. I'm asleep
but awake enough to see her sway—
a liquid dance with the wind—
and the wind becomes a phantom
made of whiskey and steam.
Through drowsy eyes I see her
roll back her head and open her mouth
to drink him in, and I hear an owl
in my throat—I'm trying to cry Stop,
but why should my mother
listen to me now? She's a lipstick smudge,
a thirsty moan, a floe
wanting nothing from life
but to melt. I press my face
against the wall and dream
of breaking levees, houses that drift
out to sea—plaster damp

with the phantom's scent. My eyes
are closed, yet I see him plume
across my world, dark and bright
as oil. He'll kill my mother first,
and then my knees will bend—
in the end, I'll marry him.
I know this even after the wind dies down
and I wake a grown woman,
flushed and queasy but safe
in a sun-drenched room,
every window and door
latched tight.

Mama, Just Go

I don't need honey for my throat.

Fancy you can pour over me
like sorghum on biscuits?
I'm sticky with your kisses.

Fancy you can burble up from sweet tea,
spoon me moonshine and lullabies,
fill my cup with fairy tales?

It's been a month of Sundays
since you nursed me in the vapor tent.
My lungs are healed.

I want to forget the yellow syrups—
Your sodden spirit steams through my skin,
reeking of whiskey and wisteria.

I gulp you down.
Cough you up.

Colors Distinguish Themselves

*Colors distinguish themselves
clearly from one another
only in the light;
in passing into the shadow
they grow weaker and disappear.*
—Jacques Maroger

Secret Sister

i.

Secret Sister came from some other father.
This explained why the sun shone
right through her. She glittered about
like one of those iridescent birds
from *National Geographic*
who blunders into Walmart. She sang
colors instead of words. Our mother
could not pronounce her name.

Her daddy was a motor thrum—a vibration in the air—
so tall you might say his head brushed

the color of distance—he wore faded jackets—
denim caps—he wore her frown—

the troubled eyes—his pockets crooned
with lonely coins—never enough

he was a voice in a smoky room—breath
sliding through a trombone—or fingers

strumming an electric sitar—all buzz
& tremble—a transatlantic call—or

a sonic boom—a thunder god—a Thunderbird—
revving engine—pointed fins

& a curled lip—a push from shore—
a rope uncoiling—footprints huge as boats—

he was the rising tide—a snare drum splash
& swish—always the rocking sky

ask him why the sky is blue
he'd say shattered waves of light

scoop his words into a Mason jar—
where'd the color go? he was

the saxophone cry of a departing plane—
she never got to meet him.

iii.

Our mother did not need
a plane to fly. Thrashing thick arms,
she careened over Walmart Plaza
& swam against the wind.

Gravity grabbed her by the hair—
tossed her back in bed.

iv.

How would you like to return?
Secret Sister asked before dinner,
the two of us in the kitchen,
peeling words over the sink.

Something avian, she went on
as though I,
the earth-bound sister,
could arrange her
reincarnation—

Not a flamingo, she decided
despite the color
of her nail polish,
but something buoyant
with working wings.

v.

Gravity meant nothing
to Secret Sister. Dozing
on a ne'er-do-well cloud,
she paddled manicured hands
& drifted past Lord & Taylor.
When the current swelled,
she became a whirling scrap of foil.

vi.

Secret Sister wore metallic lipstick
because her name was gold,
just as mine was gray—
an unfortunate blend,
dark & light together,
which explains why
she called me by my initials.
The letters pinged
like silver spoons.

vii.

We lived in a house of glass.
At night anyone walking by
might see us flutter inside,
fireflies in a jar.

Our mother drank always
from a clear round glass
a ball of honey fire
with a single cube of ice
sharp cold corners
curved glass walls

she drank always quickly
from the same round glass
a planet made of vapor
honey lava spinning
hot Saturn rings

she drank the flames always
then she drank the fumes
drank to the frozen core
ice cube swirling
corners wearing smooth

she said she was a planet
steaming at the rim
she tipped her glass higher
swallowed down the ice
the melting came so fast.

ix.

Night after night
we pressed our ears to secrets
& heard our mother stitching
tight blue minutes &
owl screeches across the floor &
the crumbling moon &
a sudden wind repeating
This can't go on

Then a suitcase snapping &
frogs foot-falling on the stairs—
always the shriek
of hinges—

x.

Nights my father didn't come,
our mother turned down the roast
& set out crayons. Secret Sister peeled the rind
from a color called flesh. I chose azure
like his Air Force ring. Mother
stood at the window & blew smoke
into the yellow light. *He's always late*
Secret Sister said. Her crayon squeaked
something hidden at the top
of a folded page. I filled the space
below the crease, completing a drawing
I could not see. We opened it to reveal
a clown with scales & serpent wings.
Melting wax & burning meat.

xi.

Secret Sister wore a purple scarf
around her neck. It helped the notes come out
indigo, which carried the aroma of wine
& chewing gum. She wore a bracelet that chimed
& an opal ring flecked with whispers.
She poured the whispers into her diary
& locked the leather tongue.

August turned thirsty & our mother
could not bear the heat. With her palette knife,
she snapped Sister's diary wide.
Cerulean spilled out, then fuchsia.
Crimson flew up & scuttled against
the window screen. We could not help
what happened next. Secret Sister
swam across a sky by Marc Chagall,
floated to an island by Gauguin,
tip-toed through a forest
by Henri Rousseau. She kissed a boy
from another frequency.

xiii.

We heard her whisper blue words
& heard a deeper voice answer azure.
Ooo—oooo—blue-azure—
like owls in the sycamore,
turning sounds into waves of light & then—
kiss-kiss-kiss—She kissed a boy
made of vibrations. Their secret language
blew through the leaves & trembled
the house. Who could sleep? Our mother
stepped onto the balcony & threw a slipper
into the wisteria. A gust of fireflies rose.

Missing from the box,
halfway between blue & green,
the crayon I need to draw
our sectional sofa with its ocean
of corded cushions—

Not the murky ocean
of Winslow Homer,
but farther south,
a Gauguin sea
tossed with psychedelic pillows

like electric fishes
in the watery space of a room
wall-to-walled not-green—

& the lava lamp.
The spoon-shaped chair.
The pinch-pleated drapes—

ceiling-to-floor paradise,
with a pull-cord that whistled
like a dolphin—*Turquoise!*

Such a slippery word—
Listen how it swishes & curls
as the lost color rolls
toward the rim of the world.

Secret Sister sent us letters
with foreign stamps—
On paper thin as cellophane,
she wrote stippled colors
too exotic to understand.
Fandango-jasmine-mauve—
which might explain why mountains turn
translucent in the rain—
or else *heliotrope-jade-vermilion*,
revealing where minutes go
when clocks wind down.

xvi.

She reached the age
of invisibility—
acquired the power
to drift unnoticed
through dress shops
& convention halls,
a Marvel Comics character,
caped.

She slipped through eyelashes
& under doors,
wearing nothing
but her scent—
no need for lipstick
or permission.

xvii.

I never thought I could fly
until night rose to the tip of the flagpole
& flooded the school.
Up I went, over the chain link fence
& the athletic field,
over eleven boys in glowing
helmets. *Don't wake yet,*
Secret Sister said.
You're learning to float—
perfecting your stroke.

xviii.

We trace our fingers over her letters
& feel the colors burn & chill.
Sometimes they darken into an
Old Master's still life—dead pheasant,
withered pear. We worry, but
always the envelope wafts lavender.
Her return address is violet,
which our mother says
has an exclusive wavelength:
790 Terahertz, located at the end
of the spectrum of light.

xix.

Drowsy from the scent of acetone,
I try to give her a manicure
while she dozes in her hospital room.

Her knotted fingers are driftwood
on the rumpled sheets, her nails
hard & ribbed like scallop shells.

In the flicker from the television,
we're a dark & mottled pair.
The sandpaper file whispers our names.

I remember the two of us
in matching dresses, posing
for our mother's camera & then

pulling away. We came from
different fathers, different worlds.
But look at us now—time-worn

like ocean-tossed things
washed onto the same bleached dune.
She raises a hand to the lamp.

Is it true that fingernails grow
in the afterlife, or do they only seem longer
with the ebbing of the flesh?

I push at ragged horizons.
Pale half-moons rise.

Light Has a Solid and Opaque Appearance

*Light has a solid and opaque appearance
whereas shadow is fluid
and transparent.*
                        —Jacques Maroger

Lobster for Lunch (21 x 30, Acrylic)

After Mexico and before she died, my mother painted
a middle-aged couple in tie dye, seated in a tropical pavilion,

confronting a lobster. The lobster spreads its crimson legs
toward three papayas and a furry coconut. A pineapple

sends up spires. It's a mystery why my mother gave
the lobster such huge claws and the people no hands.

Their impassive faces ask, *Who will slice the fruit?*
Who will open the shell?

The tourists might be my mother and one of the men
she almost married. The monkey drowses at the edge,

fondling an empty glass and a half-peeled banana.
He has my mother's nimble fingers.

Girl Playing Paganini (Charcoal on Vellum)

Alone on the glowing stage,
an other-worldly creature in black satin
chin-grips her instrument, fondles the strings,
and raises the bow. The way a spider
glides across a wall, stops and shudders,
then unfurls a silver thread from its core,
she releases the delirious notes
with jabbing elbows and nimble strokes—
an astonishing synchronicity of savagery
and beauty. I swoon in the shadows,
white roses spilling from my arms.
She whooshes past, swinging her violin
by its neck.

Killing Mr. Big

The old tom sank his claws and tried to leap
from the steel counter, but I held his scruff

and nodded to the vet who murmured, *For the best*,
because Mr. Big sprayed the house with blood

and urine and I couldn't go on
forcing expensive pills down his throat

only to find them on my pillow, coated with dust
and hardened spittle. The needle slid

beneath matted fur. Yellow eyes
saw through me to a darker me—

a woman who could hurry to her father,
stroke his hair, and approve another dose

of morphine. *He's out of pain*, the doctor said,
although we both knew the relief was mine.

Mercy and expediency—
squabbling like weary lovers

who tell so many lies, keep so many secrets,
and sleep with legs entwined.

Slugs

Every day they quadruplefy. My mother
finds them eating her Dorothy Benedict hostas,
which have puckered blue leaves and cost $200
at the horticultural fair, so she shoots them
with squirts of ammonia fired from a plastic pistol.
They're always copulating—
switching their sexes to and fro, peppering the mulch
with infinitesimal eggs. My stepfather draws a graph
to show the rise and fall of slug empires
concealed in the moist bed by the pool.
And, beneath our Persian carpets? Forty years
of secrets. I should confess:
I've left my teaching job, driven away
a decent husband, and pursued a romance
with a woman. Mother comes in from the garden,
limping from the want of new knees,
sits beside my stepfather, and ponders his ragged rows
of numbers. If I wait long enough, they'll die
and I won't have to tell.

Woman Reflecting (Watercolor & Gouache)

They need our help, these mirror folk
flopping from their frames the moment
we turn off the lights. They try so hard,
bouncing against dark windows, not sure
which side to part their hair.

Where does yours go at night?

Buttons askew, it wanders the polished halls
of your elementary school, slips behind
your childhood desk, and sits with folded hands.
Stretching tall and twice as thin, it tries to read
books made of palindromes.

In the dark it resembles you.

A Lady on NPR Says Her Brain Has a Hole the Size of a Hollyhock

But, Sister—yours is more like a peony,
a feathered swirl of misunderstandings—
a lost key. A wrong turn. Fortnightly visits
from our grandmother, who died years ago.
How long have you wandered the garden
without your left shoe? Amazing to watch
the Rubra Plena unfurl: a blood bank
of double blooms, floppy-limbed,
unmanageable as the dolls you used to cradle.
Horticulturalists suggest stakes
to support the fragile stems. Doctors
recommend a gated facility.
The lady on the radio has learned
to love her hollyhock—a stunning vacancy,
half docile, half wild.

What the Monkey Says

It's true: I've got my fingers in everything,
pulling parakeets from blue air, turning olives
into peonies. A train arrives—Your mother paints you
a new father. The world is dark and bright, strange,

familiar: an alchemy of light, shadow,
and walnut oil. Every day you eat *trompe l'oeil*
grapes. Delicious, yes? Listen: The formula
is made with Silly Putty. Nothing holds

its shape. Sure as an apricot swells and shrivels,
the surface will give way. Notice how spider milk
wicks across the canvas. A goose sheds
gray feathers, a peach opens at the seam. Oh dear—

Have I made you sad? Here—have a banana. The skin
is false, but go ahead—pinch a corner. *Peel.*

Simulcast

I am my stepfather's son:
I am an old woman. Shadows
darken his hospital room where,
in his dementia, he imagines
I am the child who died
before my birth. The difference—
nine months. Time enough for me to fly
cross-country, one womb to another,
and grow into the Air Force pilot my stepfather sees
when he looks at me.

Supposing I told my mother:
I'm me, but not me. I think she'd carry on
painting her paintings, knowing
nothing real is solid, but formed
from semi-transparent glazes,
each layer revealing
the layer below. How else to explain why
when she brought home this new father,
I recognized his voice, clung to his stories
with dizzy adoration? Love

is energy. Energy can't be destroyed,
only passed along—a secret
whispered ear to ear. Look
how his television plays a thousand shows
simultaneously. Look
how his hands reach
to find the channels—

Still Life with Oranges (22 x 18, Oil)

Jacqueline who lies beneath the glaze, blurred or turned
into a seedless fruit: Your mother did not erase you.
See how carefully she painted the shadows. How many
divorces behind a working marriage? Your eyebrows drawn
and drawn again while you squirmed on the model's stool
and tried not to breathe. Do you remember
the report from school? All those Ds
written in red. A navel orange is a sweet mutation,
sprouted from an ancient bitter tree. One stroke to turn
a D into a B, but the D doesn't go away. There you are,
like the face under van Gogh's *Patch of Grass*, cheekbones
a scaffold for revision. Someday oil and pigment
will part ways to reveal the child who
could not sit still. Mother said every navel orange
has another orange inside.

When the Last of Them Died

When the last of them died
the secret of their marvelous method
disappeared.
                    —Jacques Maroger

Perspective Dreaming

Things that happened long ago
should seem far away.
Birds become checkmarks on a painted sky,
houses shrink to dots on a distant hill.
But whenever I enter a smoky room,
I conjure you in chiseled detail—
ragged fingernails,
sleep-tousled hair.
As though you never left, I see myself
set out the old chipped mugs
I threw away years ago.
You light a cigarette,
I pour the tea,
and suddenly the room begins to sing—
The gingham curtains!
The tarnished spoons!
In the foggy light of this remembered morning
the kettle whistles the high, clear notes
of a train long vanished
around the bend.

Southbound

i.

On the last day, my stepfather asked for mushroom soup
and fed himself with a trembling spoon. Woven ferns parted,
a blue lady whispered: *Go slow.* And so he slowed,
slow as the southbound train from Lorton,
nine hundred miles of slow. *We don't want you to vibrate,*
she said, as we jostled stop to stop. *We don't want you
to aspirate,* she said, but silver walls shivered and December
clouded sunset windows like cataracts as he tried to steady
his plastic bowl. *Where are we now?*

ii.

Every Christmas we boarded the Auto Train, our car in freight,
us in coach, presents rattling in overhead bins.
Beyond fiber ferns, dusk gloomed over Occoquan Bay.
Fellow passengers murmured—
We heard the murmurs like lapping waves but couldn't see
through the ferns. We only knew that we all headed south
and soon we'd shuck our shoes and abandon them on the beach
like nautilus shells. At happy hour we might encounter
our fellow travelers out on the salty pier, sipping margaritas
through crystal straws, and we'd recognize them at once
even though we'd never met, not really. He requested a straw.
He sipped another nine hundred miles of slow, asking,
Where did you park the car?

iii.

Every December we journeyed south, just the two of us
left in a family that died. Holiday lights
flickered from Victorian porches, Richmond passed
like a camera flash, his hair frosted on the pillow.
What channel is this?

iv.

Every Christmas we traveled coach, half-sleeping
through two Carolinas, ice snapping under iron wheels,
ocean dreams hissing through turquoise gills,
and when we rolled into Florence, the town lit up
the name of his first wife—the wife who had the baby that died
and who drank herself to him. Bones melted into tweeded seats,
mushrooms hummed through ceiling vents. *My son is on board.*
Did you see him? Behind billowing ferns, a stranger peeled
an orange. Citrus strummed through ceiling vents.
Soon, very soon, we might meet in an orange grove
or a hotel lobby with mermaid fountains,
you never know who you'll discover in tropical places. People
are so much friendlier without overcoats. Maybe he'd be there,
All grown up, in an Air Force uniform. A blue lady brought blankets,
heartbeat wheels throbbed, a blue lady brought pills.

v.

Every December we departed, nine hundred miles southbound,
presents shifting in luggage racks, patients jostling
in overhead bins, our reflections bouncing on midnight
windows. Who would've thought darkness could shine
so brightly? Seventeen hours to Sanford, sometimes longer,
swaying on a solitary track, tremoring on a train that lurched
from stop to stop, waiting for a train that often halted
to make way for other trains and patients we never saw
but might meet on a steamy veranda,
like the fisherman in New Smyrna who paid our tab,
for no reason. *Where are we now?*
Presents trembled in luggage bins, Lake Moultrie
glimmered blackly, coffee sloshed from cardboard cups.

vi.

Don't let me sleep through Sanford—His arms swayed
like Spanish moss. Gray hands traced our route across
an astral map: *Moncks Corner, Goose Creek, Yamasee.*
The names glistened in the air. *Where did you park the car?*
We crossed into Georgia, a charcoal smudge,
and somewhere in the Savannah Refuge the blue lady burst
through a halogen halo. A mechanical voice drifted down—
regret the inconvenience. Metal screeched against metal—
too many patients—Mushroom lips opened and closed—
must clear the track—When the coach door whooshed open,
we saw Florida shimmer on the rim like an orange rind,
perhaps we even smelled it, but the gurney jolted
onto a chilly platform. We were in Jesup,
still in goddamn Georgia.

These old trains, so slow and inefficient, so many delays, so many
detours. Steel squealed over linoleum rails, the ocean hissed
from a heavy tank, seashells rattled in overhead bins, wheels
clattered inside his throat: *Sanford soon, Sanford soon, San—*
Nine hundred miles from Florida, the blue lady brought papers
to sign and sent me into the concrete morning. Desolate footfalls
echoed through nine hundred layers of gray. *Where am I?*
What channel is this? Where did I park the car?

After Hours of Driving, I Find It
at the Bottom of a Cul-de-Sac

—A modernist house,
all glass and steel and trapezoids,
bright as a chip of ice.

I idle at the curb and swear I hear
cocktail laughter jingle above the zigzag roof.
I'm a child again, watching my parents
glide up and down Escher stairs.

Their festive guests shimmer
through transparent doors,
flooding turquoise rooms with frozen light
like fossil fireflies.

The remembered scent of smoke and olives
drifts across the empty patio.
Ice cubes ping, glasses chime,
amber voices call me in.

Stopping by the Columbarium on a Sunny Afternoon

"We'd invite you in," my mother said, "but where
would we put you?" I must have seemed enormous
squatting before her door, third drawer from center.

If not for the nameplate, I might've seen
a diorama of Jacobean chairs, tiny forks and spoons,
and my stepfather's bonsai.

"There's barely enough room for the two of us,"
my mother went on. Deep inside the granite walls,
my stepfather growled, "I blame the Realtor."

Dogwoods fluttered, casting stained blossoms
into the fountain. Down the hill, a procession of bagpipes
let out a skirl. "She promised us a view," my mother shrilled.

I think my parents imagined themselves still
at the retirement home, rolling along a tulip-edged path
from the Independent Wing, past Assisted Living,

over to Memory Care, where the Admissions Lady
touched my arm and whispered, "Don't worry.
We'll help them downsize."

I wanted to tell my parents: There are no Realtors
at Arlington Cemetery, not with all the iron gates
and white-gloved guards holding bayonets.

A tall blue lieutenant, stiff as tin, watched me now.
In his withering gaze, I felt myself become a trinket
in a cereal box, a biscuit crumb, a cool, floating ash—

small enough to slip through a marble seam. "Wipe your feet,"
my mother called. Above the drone of bagpipes,
her vacuum began to hum.

Notes

French painter and scholar Jacques Maroger (1884-1962) believed that Rubens, Van Eyck, and other early artists had developed versatile oil-based mediums that enhanced the color and luminosity of their paintings. The mediums, he said, allowed artists to apply colors in nearly transparent glazes, achieving amazing depth and *trompe l'oeil* illusions. Working as Technical Director of the Louvre Laboratory, Maroger analyzed historic paints and tried to recreate the long-lost recipes. He later taught at the Maryland Institute in Baltimore, where he inspired a generation of students to grind colors and mix paint mediums according to historic formulas.

Made with black oil, mastic varnish, and lead, Maroger's painting mediums were temperamental. Incorrect preparation hastened deterioration of the paint. Some critics said that Maroger's research was flawed and that using the mediums would darken colors. However, painters who rebelled against the abstract expressionism of the day were drawn to Maroger's call for a return to realism.

Maroger's research and the formulas he claimed to have rediscovered are documented in *The Secret Formulas and Techniques of the Masters* by Jacques Maroger (translated by Eleanor Beckham, Studio Publications, 1948). Factory-made mediums based on Maroger's recipes can be purchased at art supply stores and online.

Several poems in this collection respond to paintings by the poet's mother, who studied Maroger's methods and experimented with his formulas. However, the characters and situations described herein are a fanciful mix of dreams, memories, and far-flung invention.

Acknowledgments

Some poems in this collection first appeared, often in different forms, in the following publications. The author gratefully acknowledges the editors and their teams.

The Asheville Poetry Review — "I Heard a River Downstairs"

Chautauqua — "My Grandmother Won't Say Why She Jumped Off the Pier" (originally titled "After the Proposal") and "Secret Sister" section xiv (originally titled "Missing from the Box")

Main Street Rag Anthologies — "After Hours of Driving, I Find It at the Bottom of a Cul-de-Sac" (originally titled "Stopping by My Childhood Home") in *Creatures of Habitat*; "Waiting for 5:00 at Bailey's Pub" (originally titled "Waiting for 5:00 at Bailey's Pub & Grill") and "Still Life with Stuffed Olive" (originally titled "Obloquy to an Olive") in *Of Burgers & Barrooms*

Mid-American Review — "Secret Sister" sections i, vi, xi, xii, xiii, xv, and xviii (originally titled "790 Terahertz")

New Ohio Review — "Stopping by the Columbarium on a Sunny Afternoon" (originally titled "At the Columbarium")

Nimrod International Journal — "Maroger's Magic," "Old Woman with Goose," "Simulcast," "Slugs," "Southbound," "The Temperature Reaches 102" (originally titled "When the Temperature Reaches 102"), and "Woman Reflecting" (originally titled "Reflections")

Pembroke Magazine — "Mama, Just Go" (originally titled "Southern Comfort")

Pilgrimage Magazine — "Secret Sister" sections iii, v, and xvii (originally titled "Flight Patterns")

Quiddity International Literary Journal — "Cocktails on the Patio, 1964" (originally titled "Drowning in Paradise")

r.kv.r.y. quarterly — "The Absinthe Drinker" (originally titled "White Lightning")

Salamander Magazine — "Killing Mr. Big" and "Secret Sister" section x (originally titled "The Folded Paper Game")

Stone Canoe Journal — "House Beautiful" and "Beware the Pearly Gates"

Water~Stone Review — "Perspective Dreaming" and "Secret Sister" section xix (originally titled "Visiting Hours")

World Enough Writers / Concrete Wolf — "Thirst" in *Last Call: The Anthology of Beer, Wine & Spirits Poetry*

"Killing Mr. Big" was nominated for a Pushcart Prize by the editor of *Salamander Magazine* in 2017.

"Maroger's Magic" and related poems under the title "Trompe l'oeil" were Jeffrey E. Smith Editor's Prize Finalists at *Missouri Review* in 2016.

"Old Woman with Goose" was a Pablo Neruda Prize Finalist at *Nimrod International Journal* in 2016.

"Secret Sister" sections i, vi, xi, xii, xiii, xv, and xviii (originally titled "790 Terahertz") was a Fineline Competition Finalist at *Mid-American Review* in 2015.

The quotes that begin each section are derived from: Maroger, Jacques. *The Secret Formulas and Techniques of the Masters*. Trans. Eleanor Beckham. New York: Studio Publications, 1948. Print.

"To My Tongue" is loosely modeled after the poem "Smell!" by William Carlos Williams.

"The Absinthe Drinker (Egg Tempera & Oil)" draws inspiration from Tim Seibles, whose poem "First Kiss" expresses the dizzy exuberance of a young, love-struck narrator.

"Mama, Just Go" draws inspiration from Carolyn Forché, who uses a similar narrative approach in her poem, "The Morning Baking."

About the Author

Jackie Craven combines a career in journalism with whimsical and often surreal writings for literary publications. Her chapbook, *Our Lives Became Unmanageable* (Omnidawn, 2016), won the publisher's Fabulist Fiction Award. Her poems have appeared in *Columbia Poetry Review, New Ohio Review, Nimrod, River Styx, Salamander, Spillway, Water~Stone Review, Women's Studies Quarterly*, and elsewhere. *Secret Formulas & Techniques of the Masters* (Brick Road Poetry Press, 2018) is her debut poetry collection. In her other lives, Jackie has worked as a travel writer, old-house rehabber, college instructor, architecture columnist, and author of books on interior design. She writes at a cluttered desk beneath her mother's painting of a juggler, a monkey, and a chaise lounge drifting in midair. Visit her at JackieCraven.com.

Our Mission

BRICK ROAD

POETRY PRESS

The mission of Brick Road Poetry Press is to publish and promote poetry that entertains, amuses, edifies, and surprises a wide audience of appreciative readers. We are not qualified to judge who deserves to be published, so we concentrate on publishing what we enjoy. Our preference is for poetry geared toward dramatizing the human experience in language rich with sensory image and metaphor, recognizing that poetry can be, at one and the same time, both familiar as the perspiration of daily labor and as outrageous as a carnival sideshow.

Available from Brick Road Poetry Press

www.brickroadpoetrypress.com

Rising to the Rim by Carol Tyx

Treading Water with God by Veronica Badowski

Rich Man's Son by Ron Self

Just Drive by Robert Cooperman

The Alp at the End of My Street by Gary Leising

The Word in Edgewise by Sean M. Conrey

Household Inventory by Connie Jordan Green

Practice by Richard M. Berlin

A Meal Like That by Albert Garcia

Cracker Sonnets by Amy Wright

Things Seen by Joseph Stanton

Battle Sleep by Shannon Tate Jonas

Lauren Bacall Shares a Limousine by Susan J. Erickson

Ambushing Water by Danielle Hanson

Having and Keeping by David Watts

Assisted Living by Erin Murphy

Credo by Steve McDonald

Also Available from Brick Road Poetry Press

www.brickroadpoetrypress.com

Dancing on the Rim by Clela Reed

Possible Crocodiles by Barry Marks

Pain Diary by Joseph D. Reich

Otherness by M. Ayodele Heath

Drunken Robins by David Oates

Damnatio Memoriae by Michael Meyerhofer

Lotus Buffet by Rupert Fike

The Melancholy MBA by Richard Donnelly

Two-Star General by Grey Held

Chosen by Toni Thomas

Etch and Blur by Jamie Thomas

Water-Rites by Ann E. Michael

Bad Behavior by Michael Steffen

Tracing the Lines by Susanna Lang

About the Prize

BRICK ROAD
POETRY PRESS

The Brick Road Poetry Prize, established in 2010, is awarded annually for the best book-length poetry manuscript. Entries are accepted August 1st through November 1st. The winner receives $1000 and publication. For details on our preferences and the complete submission guidelines, please visit our website at www.brickroadpoetrypress.com.

Winners of the Brick Road Poetry Prize

2016
Assisted Living by Erin Murphy

2015
Lauren Bacall Shares a Limousine by Susan J. Erickson

2014
Battle Sleep by Shannon Tate Jonas

2013
Household Inventory by Connie Jordan Green

2012
The Alp at the End of My Street by Gary Leising

2011
Bad Behavior by Michael Steffen

2010
Damnatio Memoriae by Michael Meyerhofer

CPSIA information can be obtained
at www.ICGtesting.com
Printed in the USA
LVHW010427271118
598372LV00001B/213/P

9 780997 955958